thelwell's.
GYMKHANA

thelwell's
GYMKHANA

Mandarin

THELWELL'S GYMKHANA

First published in Great Britain in 1979 by Eyre Methuen Ltd
Reprinted in 1981, 1985, 1986, 1987

This edition published 1991 by Mandarin Paperbacks
an imprint of Reed Consumer Books Limited
Michelin House, 81 Fulham Road, London SW3 6RB
and Auckland, Melbourne, Singapore and Toronto

Reprinted 1992, 1993, 1994 (twice)

ISBN 0 7493 0983 0

A CIP catalogue record for this book
is available from the British Library

Copyright © 1979 by Norman Thelwell

Printed and bound in Great Britain
by Cox & Wyman Ltd, Reading, Berkshire

CONTENTS

NOW YOU ALL KNOW, OF COURSE,
THAT THE POINTS OF A HORSE
ARE MAIN FEATURES OF EVERY EQUINE.
BUT YOU'LL FIND IF YOU STRADDLE
A HORSE WITH NO SADDLE –
THEY ARE ALL STICKING UP ON HIS SPINE.

POINTS OF A HORSE

(WISE EQUESTRIANS ARE ADVISED TO STUDY THEM
FOR THEIR OWN SAFETY)

ASSEMBLY POINT

STARTING POINT

BOILING POINT

DANGER POINT

POINT OF DEPARTURE

POINT OF NO RETURN

BREAKING POINT

*   *   *

OH ANGELA'S TRAINING HER JUMPER
(WHEN DADDY COMES HOME HE'LL HAVE FITS)
SHE TRIED TO JUMP OVER THE BUMPER
AND KICKED HIS NEW BENTLEY TO BITS.

THE GAZEBO'S SMASHED IN THE HA HA
(THE GARDENER, I FEAR, MAY BE DEAD)
WHY DIDN'T I LISTEN TO GRANDPA
AND BUY HER A HAMSTER INSTEAD?

HOW TO TRAIN A JUMPER

PONIES OF ALMOST ANY TYPE CAN TURN OUT TO BE GOOD JUMPERS

POWERFUL HINDQUARTERS ARE A DISTINCT ADVANTAGE

AND SOUND FEET ESSENTIAL

THE MORE PONIES JUMP, THE MORE THEY SEEM TO LIKE IT

BUT MAKE SURE YOU KNOW HOW TO STOP THEM
BEFORE THEY GET OUT OF CONTROL

IF YOU BUY A READY MADE JUMPER HE MAY HAVE
DEVELOPED A STYLE WHICH YOU DO NOT PARTICULARLY LIKE

IT IS OFTEN BETTER TO BUY A COMPLETE NOVICE AND START
FROM SCRATCH

FIRST OF ALL YOU MUST GET YOUR PONY BALANCED

HE WILL NOT GET FAR OTHERWISE

THEN TEACH HIM HOW TO WALK CORRECTLY

INTRODUCE HIM TO EASY JUMPS UNTIL HE GAINS CONFIDENCE

HE WILL SOON TACKLE BIGGER OBSTACLES WITHOUT FEAR

PONIES ARE INCREDIBLY SENSITIVE TO ANY MOOD OR ATMOSPHERE

SO NEVER LOSE YOUR PATIENCE –
AND SOONER OR LATER –

YOU'RE BOUND TO BE AMONG THE PRIZES

*　　　*　　　*

SO YOU'RE PICKING A PONY FOR LORNA?
(OH MUMMY, OH DADDY, THAT'S WIZ!)
BUT PLEASE DO NOT FORGET TO INFORM HER
THAT THE ADVERTS ARE SOMETIMES A SWIZ.

"HE HAS CARRIED A CHILD AT THE SHOW", DEAR,
MAY MEAN BY THE SEAT OF HER TREWS
AND IT'S FOOD (NOT THE FENCES) I KNOW, DEAR,
THAT HE'S "NEVER BEEN KNOWN TO REFUSE".

SO YOU'RE PICKING A PONY FOR LORNA,
TO WIN HER A ROSETTE OR CUP?
THEN MAKE SURE THERE'S A LEG AT EACH CORNER
AND DO NOT LET THEM SELL YOU A PUP.

PONIES FOR SALE

"THIS PONY HAS TAKEN MANY FIRST PRIZES."

"... AN EXCELLENT LITTLE MOVER ..."

"... HAS OFTEN BEEN PLACED IN THE SHOW RING ..."

"... OWNER FORCED TO GIVE UP ..."

"... GENUINE REASON FOR SALE ..."

"... A WELL HANDLED PONY ..."

"... ABLE TO TAKE BOTH WALLS AND TIMBER ..."

"... A GOOD ALL ROUNDER ..."

"... NOT YET BROKEN ..."

"... HAS A SLIGHT BLEMISH ..."

"... AN IDEAL PONY FOR THE NERVOUS CHILD ..."

"... VERY QUIET IN THE STABLE ..."

"... AT HOME IN TRAFFIC ..."

"... WELL KNOWN AT LOCAL SHOWS ..."

"... A WALL-EYE PONY ..."

"... WELL ABLE TO COPE WITH ANY MEMBER OF THE FAMILY ..."

*   *   *

"OH LET US RIDE." THE LADIES CRIED,
  "WE'RE TIRED OF PLAYING HOCKEY.
WE CAN COMPETE AT ANY MEET
  WITH ANY OTHER JOCKEY."

SO NOW THEY GALLOP WITH THE BOYS
  IN COLOURED SILKS AND BLOUSES
AND WHEN THEY FALL AT BECHER'S BROOK
  THEY SHOW WHO WEARS THE TROUSERS.

A DAY AT THE RACES

(A TINY TOTS' GUIDE TO THE TURF)

THE HOT FAVOURITE

GETTING ON THE BLOWER

FOUR TO ONE BAR

A NURSERY HANDICAP

SPRING DOUBLE

CALL OVER

BOTH WAYS

A RACING ACCUMULATOR

A GOOD STAYER

A BOOKIE'S PITCH

LAYING THE ODDS

ALSO RAN

PHOTO FINISH

*   *   *

THE OWNER OF A PONY MUST
  BE ONE A LITTLE HORSE CAN TRUST
TO MUCK HIS STABLE OUT AT DAWN
  AND DUST HIS HAY AND WEIGH HIS CORN
AND SCRUB THE FLOOR WITH BRUSH AND HOSE
  UNTIL IT SHINES LIKE DADDY'S NOSE
AND COMB HIS MANE AND CLEAN HIS TACK
  AND WATCH FOR WARBLES ON HIS BACK.
SO THINK OF WHAT EACH SEASON BRINGS
  AND CHECK HIS EARS FOR NASTY THINGS
AND GROOM HIS COAT AND DO NOT FAIL
  TO CLEAN HIS DOCK AND PULL HIS TAIL
AND READ A BOOK OF HORSY HINTS
  AND FEEL HIS LEGS FOR SCARS AND SPLINTS
AND DRENCH HIM LEST HE SHOULD GET WORMS
  AND SEARCH HIS DRINKING TROUGH FOR GERMS
AND KEEP ALERT FOR COUGHS AND SCOUR
  AND EXERCISE HIM FOR AN HOUR.
(DON'T GET HIM COLD OR MAKE HIM SWEAT
  OR YOU MAY HAVE TO CALL THE VET)
BEFORE YOU EAT YOUR BREAKFAST HADDOCK
  MAKE SURE HE'S COMFY IN HIS PADDOCK
    THEN OFF TO SCHOOL BEFORE YOU'RE LATE –
    AND PAT HIM AS YOU PASS THE GATE.

HOW TO KEEP HIM HAPPY

NEVER CREEP UP SILENTLY BEHIND HIM
– OR YOU MAY GIVE HIM A FRIGHT

MAKE SURE YOU GIVE HIM ABOUT TWO HOURS OF STEADY EXERCISE
EVERY DAY

— BUT DO NOT KEEP HIM OUT UNTIL HE IS EXHAUSTED

GIVE HIM A COURSE OF SUPPLING EXERCISES –

AND MAKE SURE THAT HIS MUSCLES ARE WELL TONED UP

IF OUTDOOR EXERCISE IS NOT POSSIBLE —
GIVE HIS LEGS A GOOD HAND RUBBING

ENSURE THAT HIS FEET ARE KEPT PERFECTLY DRY AT ALL TIMES

EXAMINE HIS LEGS DAILY FOR SIGNS OF TROUBLE

BUT DO NOT BE TEMPTED TO OVER-BANDAGE HIM –
IT MAY OBSCURE HIS TRUE CONDITION

MAKE SURE HE CAN GET A DRINK OF WATER
WHENEVER HE WANTS ONE

AND IF HE BOLTS HIS FOOD – TRY TO SPREAD IT OUT AS
WIDELY AS POSSIBLE

DO NOT ALLOW HIM TO EAT PLANTS
WHICH MAY BE HARMFUL TO HIM

BUT PONIES LOVE NETTLES – SO WHY NOT GATHER
SOME FOR HIM FROM TIME TO TIME AND GIVE HIM A TREAT?

❊   ❊   ❊

THE CHIEF DEFECT OF MANDY KING
  WAS BAD BEHAVIOUR IN THE RING.
SHE'D GALLOP IN BEFORE THE BELL,
  DO OTHER NAUGHTY THINGS AS WELL
LIKE PUSHING SUSAN TO THE GROUND
  BECAUSE SHE'D HAD A FAULTLESS ROUND
AND GIVING PEOPLE NASTY LOOKS
  AND LETTING BOUNCER KICK LORD SNOOKS.
WHEN ASKED TO LEAVE SHE WOULD NOT BUDGE
  BUT MADE RUDE FACES AT THE JUDGE

– SO AS I'M SURE YOU WILL SURMISE,
  THEY ONLY GAVE HER SECOND PRIZE

HOW TO BEHAVE IN THE SHOW RING

ALWAYS ENTER THE ARENA WITH CONFIDENCE –
NERVOUSNESS MAY COMMUNICATE ITSELF TO YOUR PONY

DO NOT ALLOW HIM TO BE PUT OFF BY SPECTATORS –

OR CROWDED OUT BY OTHER COMPETITORS

REMEMBER TO SALUTE THE JUDGE

AND KEEP YOUR SHOW SIMPLE – YOU ARE SHOWING OFF YOUR PONY, NOT YOURSELF

DO NOT RIDE WITH YOUR EYES GLUED TO THE JUDGE

AND **NEVER** DISPUTE HIS DECISION

EXCESSIVE PRAISE OF YOUR PONY MAY SUGGEST THAT
YOU ARE NOT USED TO SUCCESS

IF YOU ARE DUE FOR A PRIZE, DO NOT BE BLASÉ ABOUT
RECEIVING IT

– AND MOST IMPORTANT OF ALL –

KEEP IN YOUR CORRECT ORDER WHEN RIDING
IN THE LAP OF HONOUR

SUE HAD A LITTLE PONY, PETE,
  WHO GALLOPED ROUND ON PEOPLE'S FEET
AND THREW HER OFF AND WOULD NOT HALT,
  WHICH WAS ENTIRELY SUSAN'S FAULT.
EQUESTRIANS (AND HORSEMEN TOO)
  GAVE GOOD ADVICE BUT SADLY, SUE
REFUSED TO DO WHAT SHE WAS TOLD
  SO FAILED TO WIN OLYMPIC GOLD.

IF SHE HAD ONLY READ THESE TIPS
  SHE MIGHT HAVE WON SOME CHAMPIONSHIPS.

RULES FOR RIDERS

PONIES ARE GREGARIOUS – SO TRY TO GIVE HIM
AS MUCH COMPANIONSHIP AS POSSIBLE

DO NOT USE FORCE TO GET YOUR OWN WAY
– HE IS STRONGER THAN YOU ARE –

SO GET HIM TO DO WHAT YOU WANT BY GENTLE PERSUASION

NEVER TRY TO THROW HIM UNLESS YOU ARE AN EXPERT

TEACH HIM TO STAND QUIETLY WHATEVER
YOU MAY BE DOING IN THE SADDLE

IF HE MAKES A MISTAKE —

REMEMBER IT IS YOUR FAULT — NOT HIS

BUT IF HE MISBEHAVES YOU MUST TAKE ACTION IMMEDIATELY

DO NOT FORGET TO LET THE MASTER KNOW YOU ARE THERE

AND SHOUT "HOLLOA AWAY" ONLY WHEN
YOU ARE QUITE SURE THE FOX HAS GONE

DO NOT FORGET TO CONTRIBUTE TO THE DAMAGE FUND

AND ALWAYS GIVE A CHEERY "GOOD NIGHT" TO
ANYONE YOU MAY MEET ON THE WAY HOME

          ✳

DADDY, THEY SAY, HAD A TERRIBLE DAY.
HE'S BEEN SLAVING AWAY SINCE DAWN
HE'S TAKEN A POWDER AND HIT THE HAY
SO DON'T RIDE OVER HIS LAWN.

MUMMY'S IN BED WITH A SPLITTING HEAD
THERE'S DINNER ALL OVER THE WALL
THE COOKER BLEW UP AND THE BUDGIE'S DEAD
SO DON'T RIDE INTO THE HALL.

GRANDMOTHER'S HIP IS GIVING HER GYP
AND GRANDFATHER'S RACKED WITH PAIN
- SO **PLEASE** DON'T GALLOP HIM UP THE STAIRS
- OR SOMEBODY MIGHT COMPLAIN.